THE GOLDEN YEARS

text: David Sandison, Michael Heatley, Lorna Milne, Ian Welch

design: Paul Kurzeja

SIENA

Welcome to The Golden Years and the kaleidoscope of events, people, places, sights and sounds which made 1973 so memorable. After six terrible years, the war in Vietnam officially ended with a peace treaty signed in Paris. While it would prove a personal triumph for the US negotiator, Henry Kissinger, and his anxious chief in Washington, hostilities would grind on and it would be more than a year before the final North Vietnamese push on Saigon would end the war for good. Meanwhile, America's boys were coming home, and President Nixon's anxiety was over the gradually unfolding sleaze of the Watergate conspiracy which he'd denied knowing about. As resignation followed dismissal and the world watched the sorry saga unfold on television.

Confronted, as they had been in 1967, by the combined might of their Arab neighbours - who attacked as they celebrated Yom Kippur, the holiest day on the Jewish calendar - the outnumbered Israelis managed to repeat their victory of the Six Day War. This time, the Arab states wreaked their revenge on Western nations who supported Israel by cutting off voital oil supplies and throwing industries into chaos.

There was chaos of a more organized sort as Britain finally found something to smile about - the wedding of Princess Anne to the dashing Captain Mark Phillips. It was almost enough to dismiss the imminent imposition of a three-day week, and the possibility that a new Council of Ireland would solve the Ulster crisis.

OK, off you go down memory lane. Before you do, a question to set you thinking: who was Rose Mary Woods, and what part did she play in the year's biggest scandal? The answer's in here, and tons more besides. Good reading!

Paris Treaty Means Vietnam Ceasefire

PROTRACTED NEGOTIATIONS at the Paris peace conference ended in an historic agreement being signed today by all parties involved in the 17-year Vietnam War. The agreement called for a ceasefire - to commence the following weekend and to be enforced by troops from neutral countries - another international conference within the next month, and a complete military withdrawal by the United States at the end of 60 days.

Not surprisingly, both sides were claiming a victory. President Nixon went on television tonight to tell the American people that US objectives have been achieved, while Hanoi's chief negotiator, Le Duc Ho (pictured with Henry Kissinger), viewed the deal as proof that 'Right has triumphed over wrong'.

Sadly they were both wrong and celebrations proved to be premature. The war would not actually end until April 1975, and the seeds of this treaty's failure could have been seen in the fact that the agreement turned out to be two separate deals.

The South Vietnam regime's refusal to recognize the Vietcong meant that two separate documents were prepared for two different signing ceremonies, one in the morning, the other in the afternoon.

UK TOP 10 SINGLES

1: Long Haired Lover From Liverpool
- Little Jimmy Osmond
2: The Jean Genie
- David Bowie
3: Hi Hi Hi/C Moon
- Wings
4: Solid Gold Easy Action
- T Rex
5: Crazy Horses
- The Osmonds
6: Ball Park Incident
- Wizzard
7: You're So Vain
- Carly Simon
8: Blockbuster
- Sweet
9: Big Seven
- Judge Dread
10: Always On My Mind
- Elvis Presley

JANUARY 11

Open University Honours First

Eight hundred and sixty seven men and women today became the first students in Britain to graduate without attending college in the conventional way when they were given their degrees by the Open University.

Prime Minister Harold Wilson's dream - of a university for all whose lack of formal qualifications previously barred them from higher education - was established in the new town of Milton Keynes, Buckinghamshire, in 1971. With no formal entry requirements, the key to Open University success was, and remains, pure hard work, often at unsociable hours at home. That regime had obviously paid off for the students who, after three years of correspondence study backed up by lectures broadcast on TV, were present for the University's first graduation ceremony.

JANUARY 30

Watergate Defendants Found Guilty

The names of two of the five men accused and found guilty of breaking into the offices of the Democratic National Committee had become household names in the United States as the story behind their trial unfolded in the media. G Gordon Liddy and James

W McCord - previously aides to the Nixon election organization - were today found guilty of burglary during their attempt to spy on the Democratic Party's Watergate headquarters during the 1972 Presidential elections. It was McCord who would

later allege that there had been a White House cover-up to suppress official involvement in the break-in, thus setting the whole Watergate show on the road, and an unravelling of events which would eventually topple President Nixon himself.

Wedding Bells For Fonda And Caine

In what was certainly a memorable month for showbusiness marriages, Jane Fonda (daughter of actor Henry, an Oscar-winning actress for *Klute*, and future aerobics guru) wed Tom Hayden, a noted anti-Vietnam politician, in Hollywood today.

Also this month, British film star Michael Caine (real name Maurice Micklewhite, and no spring chicken at 40) married model and actress Shakira Bakjish, a union that was to prove more lasting than the Fonda-Hayden alliance.

Clapton Hits Comeback Trail

Eric 'Slowhand' Clapton, perhaps the world's leading rock guitarist, celebrated his survival of a troubled period of drug dependency today by relaunching his career at London's Rainbow Theatre in the company of fellow stars Steve Winwood (Traffic), Pete Townshend (The Who), Ron Wood (The Faces) and others.

'I was very nervous, sick, the whole bit,' a tired but triumphant Eric later admitted to *Rolling Stone* magazine. Two sell-out shows saw Clapton, 27, taking his first steps towards a solo career which would endure into the 1990s – though after finding fame and fortune as a high-rolling member of The Yardbirds, Cream, Blind Faith and Derek & The Dominos, his music and lifestyle would become noticeably less extrovert.

LBJ Is Dead, Victim Of Vietnam War

FORMER US PRESIDENT Lyndon Baines Johnson (pictured) died of a heart attack today, at the age of 64. Ironically, his death came only hours before news broke of the Paris cease-fire treaty he would have given anything to have been able to negotiate himself while in office.

Johnson had suffered from heart disease for the past 18 years and had his fatal attack at his ranch in Johnson City, Texas, the town in which he grew up. The son of a farmer, he trained and worked as a high-school teacher before entering politics in President Franklin D Roosevelt's administration in 1937.

Popularly known by his initials alone, LBJ ran against John F Kennedy in the race for the 1960 Democratic Presidential nomination and, although Kennedy beat him, was chosen as his successful running mate in the Presidential election.

Vice President for the three years until Kennedy's assassination, LBJ took up the reins of office to score a number of notable achievements on the domestic front – most notably the 1964 Civil Rights Act, and reforms to cut taxes while waging war on poverty.

But LBJ was unable to negotiate a successful victory or withdrawal from Vietnam. During his time in office, the US commitment of troops increased massively, as did the level of bombing. Faced with growing widespread protests against the war and failing health, he decided not to stand again for re-election in 1968.

Concorde Rejected By US Airlines

The two largest air carriers in the United States - Pan Am and Trans World Airlines - today announced that they would not, after all, be purchasing the 13 *Concordes* which they'd planned to buy.

The US cancellation, in 1970, of its own supersonic passenger jet, the Boeing 707, had appeared to hand the initiative to the Anglo-French project, but political opposition and delays in granting *Concorde* the right to fly into US airports from Europe would sour the success of being the world's one and only supersonic passenger transport to commence and stay in regular service.

Foreman Weighs In As Champ

George Foreman the 24-year-old American heavyweight boxer, was definitely on a roll today when - having won 40 consecutive previous fights - he fought Joe Frazier for the world heavyweight title and won.

The crowd gathered to watch the fight in Jamaica didn't have long to wait either, the former Olympic heavyweight gold medallist took out the reigning champion with a knock-out in the second round.

Foreman's battles with Muhammad Ali for the right to be the undisputed world's best heavyweight were to keep him in the headlines for the next few years, and he would make a remarkable, high-profile comeback in the 1990s, while in his forties.

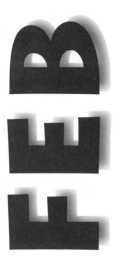

FEB

Tears And Cheers As US PoWs Return Home

THE RECENT VIETNAM peace agreement resulted in special St Valentine's Day celebrations by the families of 20 US servicemen who arrived home from captivity today, the first prisoners of war to be released by the North Vietnamese.

First to step down the gangway at Travis Air Force base in California was a naval airman, Captain Jeremiah Denton. The men were greeted with cheers, tears and emotional reunions with families some of the men were barely able to recognize after as long as eight years in detention.

It was fitting that the men should be returned via California, for they used to celebrate the arrival of good news by whistling *California Here I Come*.

The US kept its side of the peace treaty bargain by returning Vietcong prisoners to North Vietnam. By the middle of March, the prison which American PoWs had dubbed 'The Hanoi Hilton' had reportedly been emptied in the exchange.

FEBRUARY 10

Railway Threatens Liverpool Rock Venue

The Cavern Club, legendary birthplace of Merseybeat and the subterranean venue for many of The Beatles' earliest performances, was today given a three-month reprieve by British Rail.

An underground rail line was planned to run through the Matthew Street site – though owner Roy Adams was keen to preserve the room where The Fab Four made 292 performances in the early 1960s.

Ten years on, much of Matthew Street had become a car park, with no formal indication of The Cavern's presence. There was still music in the street, however - a club called *Eric's* was flourishing as a fashionable venue featuring 'new-wave' Liverpool groups like Echo and The Bunnymen and The Teardrop Explodes.

FEBRUARY 7

General Strike Shuts Down Ulster

Orchestrated by Ulster Unionists and supported by power, industrial and transport workers, a one-day general strike effectively crippled Northern Ireland today. The strike's success was due, in no small measure, to the actions of masked men who intimidated would-be strike-breakers and threatened the owners of shops who tried to remain open.

Four people were reported killed in shooting incidents, while petrol bombs reinforced the shut-or-else demands of the paramilitary enforcers. As looting spread throughout the deserted centre of Belfast, a powerless British government declared a state of emergency.

FEBRUARY 13

Moore Sighted By 9.9 Million 'Astronomers'

Television astronomer Patrick Moore's unforeseen collision in an orbit with Eamonn Andrews and his Big Red Book gave the British version of *This Is Your Life* lift-off today as it registered its biggest viewing figure to date – 9.9 million. The show, which was presented by Andrews from its UK launch in 1955 until his death in 1987, and subsequently by Michael Aspel, once achieved the longest number of consecutive years in which a programme reached No 1 in the TV ratings. And Moore - the lovable, if somewhat unkempt and seemingly disorganized presenter of BBC TV's *The Sky At Night* - was obviously a highly popular subject.

ARRIVALS

Born this month:

9: Svetlana Boginskaya, Russian Olympic gymnast

10: Dean Gordon, England Under-21 football player

DEPARTURES

Died this month:

8: Max Yasgur (owner of the New York State farm where Woodstock Festival took place), aged 53

11: Hans Jensen, German physicist, 1963 Nobel Prize winner, aged 65

22: Elizabeth Bowen, Irish writer, aged 73

FEBRUARY 13

UK Gas Workers Extinguish Wage Hopes

The British government's attempts at wage restraints in the public sector fell foul of more than one union during February. Gas workers began a nationwide strike today and, by the end of the month, they had been joined by railway workers and traditionally less strike-happy civil servants.

With the widespread power cuts of the previous year still fresh in the country's collective memory, hopes were dwindling that the Conservatives would be able to contain pay rises, although it would be a further 12 months before Prime Minister Edward Heath would call a general election in a bid to re-establish his mandate.

Israelis Down Libyan Airliner

ALL 74 PASSENGERS and crew aboard a Libyan Arab Airlines Boeing 727 airliner died today when it was shot down by Israeli jets (pictured). Initially slow to admit responsibility for the attack, it would not be until the next day that Israel's Defence Minister, General Moshe Dayan, would confirm that it had happened, and describe the action as 'an error of judgement'.

The attack on an apparently defenceless civilian aircraft was denounced as a 'criminal act' by Libya, although Israeli authorities maintained that the airliner had failed to take heed of repeated instructions to land as it flew off-course, and apparently without radio contact, over a military installation in the Sinai Desert.

This version was refuted by Egyptian ground control staff based in Cairo. They supported a Libyan claim that the aircraft's French captain – whose last words were 'we are shot by a fighter' – had not been warned. Within a fortnight the Israeli Government had agreed to pay compensation for an act which General Dayan said his country had 'no reason to feel guilty' about.

Wounded Knee Flares Up Again

Eighty-three years after the Sioux lost their famous battle with the US Cavalry at Wounded Knee, they again resorted to direct action in defence of their land and culture.

In a bid to compel the US Senate to set up an inquiry into the treatment of American Indians, 250 militant supporters of the American Indian Movement occupied a trading post and church on the Pine Ridge Sioux Reservation in South Dakota at Wounded Knee today, holding ten hostages. Shots were exchanged with US law enforcement officers, but no-one was reported hurt. The occupation of Wounded Knee would last until May, with a number of ringleaders arrested and charged with various offences.

Ali Beats Bugner In Las Vegas

British heavyweight Joe Bugner got a 12-round boxing lesson from Muhammad Ali in Las Vegas today when he lost a bruising encounter with the former world champion on points. A large contingent of British fans could not help the Hungarian-born Bugner raise his skills or strength to defeat Ali, who hampered his vision with cuts over his eyes at the beginning, and near the end, of their tussle.

MARCH 3

IRA Hits London With New Bomb Campaign

THE LAW AND THE GOVERNMENT were the targets of IRA bombs which killed one person and injured 250 in central London today. One bomb exploded outside the Old Bailey law courts (pictured), the other at the Ministry of Agriculture in Whitehall. Two more car bombs were defused in the West End after police acted on coded telephone warnings.

The bombings, which it was feared signalled the beginning of a new terror campaign on the British mainland, were timed to coincide with this week's unprecedented referendum in Northern Ireland in which the people of the Province were asked to decide whether or not they wished to remain part of the United Kingdom.

With most Catholics boycotting the March 9 referendum, the province voted 90-1 in favour of continued links.

MARCH 3

Britain Basks In Reflected Grammy Glory

Fast-rising US soul singer Roberta Flack was honoured with a pair of Grammies in New York today for her spellbinding performance of *The First Time Ever I Saw Your Face,* causing celebrations in Britain. The song, which won both Song of the Year and Record of the Year awards, was written by British folk-singer Ewan MacColl, father of future singer-songwriting star Kirsty MacColl.
British talent was also behind American singer Harry Nilsson's Best Male Pop Vocal Performance award for *Without You,* a song written by Tommy Evans and Pete Ham, both members of pop band Badfinger and both destined to commit suicide when they found themselves overwhelmed by business problems.

MARCH 20

CIA Dabbles In South American Politics

Fresh evidence of the lengths to which the Central Intelligence Agency had been willing to go in the name of US 'security' emerged in Washington today when William Merriam, Vice President of International Telephone and Telegraph (ITT), revealed that joint activities between ITT and the CIA had been designed to prevent the Marxist Salvador Allende being elected President of Chile in 1970.

The political sabotage, which included propaganda and the provocation of anti-Marxist violence against Allende's party, failed when he was elected by a landslide majority. ITT and the CIA were later found to be 'at fault' by the Senate committee investigating the workings of US-owned multinational companies.

UK TOP 10 SINGLES

1: Cum On Feel The Noize
- Slade
2: Feel The Need In Me
- The Detroit Emeralds
3: 20th Century Boy
- T Rex
4: Cindy Incidentally
- The Faces
5: The Twelfth Of Never
- Donny Osmond
6: Killing Me Softly With His Song
- Roberta Flack
7: Hello Hurray
- Alice Cooper
8: Part Of The Union
- The Strawbs
9: Power To All Our Friends
- Cliff Richard
10: Blockbuster
- Sweet

MARCH 20

Ulster Assembly Proposed

Following the result of the March 9 Ulster referendum, far-reaching new proposals for the government of Northern Ireland were unveiled today by Secretary of State Willie Whitelaw in a White Paper which spelt good and bad news for democracy in the province.

A new Assembly of 80 members was to be created, composed of both Catholics and Protestants in a coalition government based on proportional representation – an improvement on the former Protestant-dominated assembly. However, the White Paper also included plans to abolish the ideal of trial by jury, which was thought to be unworkable in Ulster because of inevitable threats to witnesses.

MARCH 27

Marlon Brando Rejects Oscar

To the amazement of Hollywood, actor Marlon Brando (pictured) tonight rejected the Oscar awarded to him as Best Actor in 1972's popular blockbuster *The Godfather.* Brando – who played a murderous mafia boss in the film – rejected the Academy Award in protest at the plight of American Indians. It wasn't the first such award Brando had won, having collected one for his portrayal of boxer Terry Malloy in *On The Waterfront* in 1954. If the producers of *The Godfather* were deprived of seeing their star accept his Oscar, they still had two awards to fall back on – the movie walked off with Best Script and Best Picture. Not everyone was impressed by Brando's gesture, however. Gregory Peck suggested Brando might help the Indians more by donating some of his substantial *Godfather* earnings to their cause.

MARCH 8

Beatle Paul In Pot Plant Palaver

Ex-Beatle Paul McCartney faced a Scottish court today and pleaded guilty to a charge of growing marijuana plants at his farm on the remote west coast Mull of Kintyre. McCartney claimed the seeds were given to him by a fan and he didn't know what they would grow into.
Surprisingly, then, McCartney's lawyer explained his client had an active interest in horticulture. Escaping with a fine on this occasion, the musician would be briefly imprisoned in Japan when marijuana was found in his luggage in 1980.

MARCH 7

Bangladesh Elects First President

Despite having become an 'independent' state in 1971, Bangladesh - formerly East Pakistan - had to wait until today to elect its first President, Sheikh Mujib Rahman, leader of the Awami (People's) League.
Sheikh Mujib had won a majority in 1970 elections, but was prevented by West Pakistan from forming a government. As a result, civil war broke out and opposition from West Pakistan was only defeated when India stepped in to support the emergent nation. Sheikh Mujib was to set up his government in the new Bangladesh capital of Dhaka.

14

Theatreland Mourns Noel Coward, The Master

THE WORLDS OF THEATRE, film and music lost one of the twentieth century's most sophisticated wits and versatile talents today with the death of Sir Noel Coward at his villa in Blue Harbour, Jamaica, at the age of 73.

Playwright, actor and songwriter Coward - popularly known as 'The Master' to his legion of friends and fans - was born in Teddington, Middlesex, and made his stage début at the tender age of ten. Sixteen years later, and with no formal musical training, he had three hit shows running in London's West End.

Coward's heyday was the period between the wars when his London stage successes included the 1929 operetta *Bitter Sweet, Private Lives* (first staged in 1930, but constantly revived to this day), and *Blithe Spirit*, a stage hit in 1941 and filmed in 1945.

His contribution to the British war effort came most notably with his writing, directing and producing the gung-ho naval epic *In Which We Serve*, and Coward was also responsible for the screenplay of the 1946 British film classic *Brief Encounter*. An internationally successful revue and cabaret performer, Coward will most famously be best remembered for his delightfully self-deprecating classic song satire, *Mad Dogs And Englishmen*.

AGE AND YOUTH SPRING SHOCKS ON 'THE STING'S OSCAR NIGHT

Although the competition for the Best Film Oscar in this year's Academy Awards was pretty tough, with the excellent rites-of-passage *American Graffiti,* Ingmar Bergman's powerful *Cries And Whispers,* the shock-horror of *The Exorcist* and the touch of class that was the adult comedy *A Touch Of Class* vying for honours, all the smart money was on *The Sting,* the Robert Redford/Paul Newman caper classic.

The smart money was right. Not only did *The Sting* emerge as Best Film, but director George Roy Hill won his category, David S Ward's screenplay secured him a statuette, William Reynolds' editing earned him his prize and the beautiful 1920s period detail of Henry Bumstead's sets earned him the Art Direction Oscar.

Composer Marvin Hamlisch proved he could do no wrong when his Scott Joplin-inspired score for *The Sting* became only one of three Oscars he'd pick up during the evening. The others were for the score he'd written for Barbra Streisand's movie *The Way We Were,* and for the title song itself, which he'd written with lyricists Alan and Marilyn Bergman.

A brief re-cap of that Oscars list for *The Sting* should advise you that the 1973 Academy Awards still had a sting of its own in its glittering tail. No Oscar for Redford or Newman? Even stranger, while Redford was nominated for the Best Actor award, Newman wasn't.

Redford lost out to an on-form Jack Lemmon, whose dramatic performance in *Save The Tiger* was enough to win him the crucial vote. The other contenders were Marlon Brando (for the scandalous *Last Tango In Paris*), Jack Nicholson (for *The Last Detail*) and Al Pacino (for the excellent *Serpico*).

Newman's wife, the redoubtable Joanne Woodward, also lost out this year. Pitted against Ellen Burstyn (the bewildered mother in *The Exorcist*), Marsha Mason (in *Cinderella Liberty*), Barbra Streisand (*The Way We Were*) and Glenda Jackson (*A Touch Of Class*), she lost out to Jackson, who returned to her Hampstead home with a match for the Oscar she'd won in 1970 for *Women In Love*.

Just as it's surprising that Paul Newman missed nomination for what was an undoubted two-hander, the omission of Jackson's *A Touch Of Class* co-star George Segal from the lists still puzzles many people.

But the real surprises came in the Supporting Actor and Actresses departments. The former went to John Houseman, a film producer and co-founder with Orson Welles of the Mercury Theatre in 1937, who was dragged

Robert Redford in The Sting

in front of the cameras to play a wicked old professor in the otherwise un-nominated *The Paper Chase*. At the age of 71, he'd won an Oscar in his screen debut, the oldest person ever so to do!

The Supporting Actress award went to the youngest-ever - 11-year-old Tatum O'Neal, who'd stolen every scene in *Paper Moon* from some serious adult actors, including her own father, Ryan.

During a ceremony disrupted by a streaker, it was fitting that the Academy should honour one of cinema's timeless comic heroes, Groucho Marx, with a Special Oscar. Such awards are usually made because the recipient is known to be near to the closing credits of an otherwise unawarded life. True, Groucho was ill and frail, but he had the last laugh. He didn't light his last cigar for another three years.

APRIL

APRIL 11

Nazi Bormann Confirmed Dead

A skeleton unearthed in Berlin was today officially identified as that of the Nazi war criminal Martin Bormann. Relatively unknown in comparison with other Nazi leaders, Bormann became Hitler's Private Secretary in 1942 and was an influential member of the inner party circle, holding considerable power and therefore bearing his share of responsibility for Nazi activities.

Bormann disappeared during the closing stages of the war, but was nevertheless found guilty at the Nuremburg Trials. Until today, it was not known whether he was dead or alive. West German officials were now finally able to close their file on the man they believed committed suicide on May 2, 1945.

APRIL 1

The VATman Cometh

Value Added Tax - or VAT for short - was introduced in Britain today, bringing with it wide-ranging effects on retailers and consumers alike. A tax on goods and services, it represented the latest step in the UK's European commitment to abolish custom duties between member states and gradually introduce a common external tariff. France, Germany, Holland, Luxembourg and Belgium had already adopted VAT, although Italy had yet to do so.

It was estimated that 1.5 million British traders would be liable to register for VAT, so giving plenty of work for the new VAT-men whose enquiries were to send many a shiver down the spines of small business men and women.

APRIL 8

India Annexes Sikkim

In a month when the Indian Government announced a campaign to save the tiger – which was in danger of extinction – it appeared to be less concerned about the independence and autonomy of the inhabitants of the tiny Himalayan country of Sikkim. Following a spate of anti-government riots, India announced it was annexing the nation, which shared a border with China.

The small Buddhist state had previously been an Indian protectorate since partition in 1947, but over the next couple of years was to suffer an increasing loss of sovereignty.

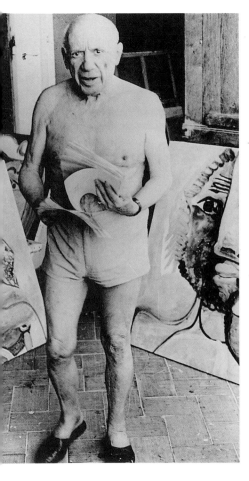

Pablo Picasso, Modern Art Master, Dies

THE CONTROVERSIAL ARTIST Pablo Picasso suffered a fatal heart attack at his house at Mougins in the South of France, today, at the age of 91. Perhaps more than any other painter, Picasso's art embraced the many and varied influences of the twentieth century in a prolific career which produced an estimated 140,000 drawings and paintings, 100,000 engravings and 300 sculptures.

Picasso was trained in art from a very young age by his Spanish father, although ironically, he was later to comment on children's paintings, 'When I was their age I could draw like Raphael. It has taken me a lifetime to learn how to draw like them'. Presumably, he felt he had to 'unlearn' what his father taught him.

He certainly spent that lifetime in search of new ideas, experimenting with what became known as his Blue and Rose paintings of circus artists, and later on Cubist, Surreal and neo-classical works.

Together with painter Georges Braque he founded the influential Cubist movement, of which his famous *Les Demoiselles d'Avignon* was the first example. The starkness of his massive painting *Guernica* depicted the atrocity which obliterated the town of that name in the Spanish civil war.

APRIL 30

White House Aides Are First Watergate Casualties

THE UNITED STATES WAS agog today as it learned of the resignation of four of President Richard Nixon's top advisers as a result of the Watergate scandal, which was now filling American and world headlines. The White House Chief of Staff, H R 'Bob' Haldeman, (pictured left) Nixon's Chief Domestic Affairs Adviser John Ehrlichman (pictured right), Attorney-General Richard Kleindienst and legal aide John Dean, all stepped down to become the first official casualties of the affair.

Forced to make a public statement, President Nixon broadcast to the nation and accepted responsibility for what had happened. He still denied that he had been involved in either the Watergate burglary or the subsequent cover-up, though he acknowledged the latter had taken place. He rounded off his speech by asking journalists to 'give me hell every time you think I'm wrong'.

Unfortunately, Nixon's speech marked a downward spiral in his popularity, which meant that from that time onwards he could do little right.

APRIL 7

Eurovision Cliff-Hanger Glues Britain To TV

The Eurovision Song Contest became Britain's most-watched TV programme of the year tonight, thanks mainly to the participation of Cliff Richard. Close on 10 million UK homes were said to have tuned in, contributing to a record total of 300 million viewers from 32 countries.

It wasn't the first time British pop's bachelor boy had taken part in the event, having finished runner-up in 1968 with *Congratulations.* And it was to be 'so near yet so far' again for Cliff in Luxembourg's Nouveau Theatre, when *Power To All Our Friends* once more came second.

The home winner, Anne-Marie David's *Tu Te Reconnaitras (Wonderful Dream),* earned unusual scorn from born-again Christian Cliff. 'I just don't like the song', he said, adding quickly, 'No, it's not sour grapes!'

APRIL 13

US TV In Rock Censorship Storm

White rhythm and blues artists The J Geils Band fell foul of US media censors tonight in what appeared to be a new wave of repression in terms of rock music lyrics. The words 'get it up' from their song *Give It To Me* were cut when they appeared on ABC-TV's prestigious *In Concert* programme.

Soul star Curtis Mayfield, hardly the most controversial of artists, also ran into trouble with *Pusherman,* his denunciation of the drugs trade, when he appeared on networked *Soul Train.* All drugs references were edited from the song – including half the first line!

APRIL 17

Afghanistan Sheds Monarchy

The Afghan monarchy was abolished today in the wake of a military coup which ousted the government and created the new Afghan Republic. The move ended 54 years of benevolent rule by a monarchy which created a written constitution four years after it first came to power in 1919.

Repeated efforts to westernize Afghanistan had met with increased opposition and it was noticeable that pro-Russian politicians became more influential following the 1973 coup – a situation that would ultimately lead to a long and bitter war between Islamic nationalist rebels and the Soviet Union.

APRIL

21

MAY 7

Watergate Journalists Honoured As Senate Starts Hearings

WITH THE FULL RAMIFICATIONS of the Watergate affair still unfolding before the eyes of an amazed public, the two journalists who played a key role in exposing the cover-up were today each awarded a Pulitzer Prize for public service in journalism.

The *Washington Post* editor Ben Bradlee could have had little idea of the consequences of assigning investigative journalists Carl Bernstein (29) and Bob Woodward (30) (pictured) to a routine investigation into an apparently innocent burglary of Democratic Party offices in 1972.

Aided by an anonymous source code-named 'Deep Throat', they gradually unravelled the web of intrigue surrounding the crime, and the implications for those at all levels in the White House. The story of the reporters' quest would be portrayed in the 1976 film *All The President's Men,* starring Robert Redford and Dustin Hoffmann, and gain a Best Writer Oscar for William Goldman.

Watergate would resume its position on the world's front pages on May 17 when a Senate select committee began its own detailed investigation into an alleged cover-up. Televised in full, the hearings would make a star of chairman Senator Sam Ervine of North Carolina.

He set the tone of the hearings, and his style, when he described the Watergate burglars as trying to steal 'not the jewels, money or other property of American citizens, but something much more valuable - their most precious heritage, the right to vote in a free election'.

MAY 29

Princess Anne Is To Marry

Despite two months of strenuous denials of a romance, Buckingham Palace today confirmed that the Queen's only daughter, Princess Anne, was to marry 24-year-old Mark Phillips, a Lieutenant in the Dragoon Guards. The couple had made their intention to marry public during the Badminton Horse Trials, where both were competing.

A professional horseman, Mark Phillips shared a passion for horses and the cross-country sport of eventing with Princess Anne. The marriage - the first for one of the Queen's four children - was to take place in Westminster Abbey on November 14 and would be transmitted live on TV worldwide.

MAY 14

NASA Launches Skylab

Science fiction became science fact today when NASA launched *Skylab,* the world's first space-based scientific research laboratory, into orbit from Cape Kennedy.

The space station was designed to stay above the Earth for two years. Later this month, the first of three crews to work on board the lab – NASA astronauts Joseph Kerwin, Paul Weitz and Charles Conrad - took off on an initial 28-day mission. Teething problems with *Skylab's* vital solar power panels meant that the crew were carrying excess baggage, in the form of replacements, when they blasted off on May 25.

MAY 18

Heath Slams 'Unacceptable' Lonrho

Three days after Lonrho - the British owned international mining and trading company - was criticized in a High Court hearing for its use of tax havens and ownership of a £350,000 company house, Prime Minister Edward Heath faced searching questions today in the House of Commons about past links between former cabinet ministers and the industrial giant. Choosing his words carefully, Mr Heath stressed that Lonrho's activities and style did not, in his opinion, typify British industry. Then, in what was destined to become an historic phrase, he said Lonrho was 'an unpleasant and unacceptable face of capitalism'.

UK TOP 10 SINGLES

1: Tie A Yellow Ribbon Round The Old Oak Tree
- Dawn
2: Hell Raiser
- Sweet
3: See My Baby Jive
- Wizzard
4: Hello Hello I'm Back Again
- Gary Glitter
5: Drive-In Saturday
- David Bowie
6: Giving It All Away
- Roger Daltrey
7: Brother Louie
- Hot Chocolate
8: And I Love You So
- Perry Como
9: My Love
- Paul McCartney & Wings
10: No More Mr Nice Guy
- Alice Cooper

MAY 24

Ministers Resign In New British Sex Scandals

BRITAIN'S CONSERVATIVE government was rocked today by sex scandals which forced the resignations of two senior ministers – the Lord Privy Seal, Earl Jellicoe, who was also Leader of the House of Lords, and Lord Lambton (pictured), the Under-Secretary for Defence.

The Secret Service had been keeping tabs on both men since it was discovered that they were associating with known prostitutes but, having ascertained that neither affair constituted a breach of security, the details of the ministers' questionable private lives had remained under wraps.

Unfortunately, for the government, the husband of call-girl Norma Levy sold compromising photos of Lord Lambton to the newspapers, thereby making the scandal public and precipitating the resignations.

Pressed for a statement in the House of Commons today, a clearly embarrassed Prime Minister, Edward Heath, stressed his confidence in a Security Commission report which verified that neither of his disgraced colleagues had been involved in security lapses or blackmail attempts.

MAY 26

That's Life... as We Know It!

Britain's longest-running and most influential consumer affairs programme *That's Life* hit the nation's TV screens tonight on BBC1. Presented by Esther Rantzen, a former production assistant on the news magazine *Man Alive,* and one-time sidekick to Bernard Braden, the nation's former consumer's champion, *That's Life* would go on to become the longest-running show of its type on UK television.

Characters thrown up by the show during nearly two decades on screen included Cyril Fletcher, inventor of the 'Odd Ode', comedy actor George Layton, singer-songwriter Doc Cox (who had *risqué* UK hits with the alias Ivor Biggun) and a succession of performing animals and obscenely shaped vegetables.

MAY 5

Wearside Wonders Scoop FA Cup Prize

Second Division Sunderland pulled off one of the biggest Cup Final upsets of the century today by beating the top-ranked Leeds United, thanks to a single goal from Ian Porterfield and some breathtaking goalkeeping by Jim Montgomery.

Managed by the flamboyant Don Revie, the formidable Leeds side were expected to win English football's showpiece fixture at a canter. But Sunderland, managed by the veteran Bob Stokoe, held on against relentless pressure from star Leeds strikers. Jim Montgomery's double reflex save of thunderbolt shots by Cherry and Lorimer would be replayed in TV highlights more times than the winning goal.

Sunderland's was the first FA Cup win by a Second Division club for 42 years. Goalscorer Porterfield would later enjoy a second career in management with Aberdeen, Reading and Chelsea.

MAY 6

Simon Sings Solo (Where's Artie?)

Singer-songwriter Paul Simon played Boston Music Hall tonight. Nothing unusual in that...except that he was opening his first tour since splitting from his lanky singing partner Art Garfunkel, with whom he performed hits like *Mrs Robinson* and *Bridge Over Troubled Water.* To keep him company on stage, Simon enlisted Latin American quartet Urubamba and gospel group The Jesse Dixon Singers. The tour would be recorded for the 1974 album release, *Live Rhymin'*.

JUNE

JUNE 7

Brandt Makes Historic Visit To Israel

Nearly thirty years after the end of World War II, feelings between Germans and Jews were still acutely sensitive as West German Chancellor Willy Brandt discovered when he paid a historic visit to Israel. Herr Brandt, born in Lubeck, played an active role in the anti-Nazi Resistance Movement during the war, a fact that escaped the attention of the 200 hundred or so young protesters who dubbed him a 'German murderer' when he arrived in Jerusalem.

Brandt was greeted by the Israeli Defence Minister, Moshe Dayan, and Prime Minister Golda Meir who welcomed him to the country 'with the esteem due to one who, in the darkest period for the human race and especially for the Jewish people, joined forces with those who fought the Nazis'.

It appeared to have been a moving experience for the Chancellor, who paid public tribute to the six million Jewish victims of the concentration camps.

JUNE 8

Powell Gives Pithy Poll Pointer

The maverick Conservative Member of Parliament Enoch Powell surpassed himself today when he suggested that the public should vote for the opposition Labour Party to avoid Britain's entry to the European Economic Community, or Common Market.

It was only the latest in a series of controversial Powell pronouncements – and one sure to enrage Prime Minister Edward Heath, who'd sacked Powell from a junior finance minister's post in 1968 after he called for stronger immigration controls, quoting Virgil's

vision of 'the Tiber foaming with blood' if his warnings were not heeded.

Powell would leave the Conservative Party later in the decade, after entry to the EEC had gone ahead against his wishes, but would remain a voice in Parliament as an Ulster Unionist.

JUNE 26

New Terror Group Emerges In Ulster

A new terrorist faction emerged in war-torn Northern Ireland today - the Ulster Freedom Fighters.

A Loyalist vigilante group, they claimed responsibility for several sectarian murders in the Province, predicting 'there will be more'. Their actions had only served to increase the level of violence, as IRA gunmen shot dead a Pakistani shopkeeper who dared to serve tea and sandwiches to British troops in what appeared to be nothing more or less than a 'tit-for-tat' response.

UK TOP 10 SINGLES

1: Can The Can
- Suzi Quatro
2: Rubber Bullets
- 10cc
3: See My Baby Jive
- Wizzard
4: One And One Is One
- Medicine Head
5: Albatross
- Fleetwood Mac
6: And I Love You So
- Perry Como
7: The Groover
- T Rex
8: Stuck In The Middle With You
- Stealer's Wheel
9: Tie A Yellow Ribbon Round The Old Oak Tree
- Dawn
10: Walking In The Rain
- The Partridge Family

Soviet Supersonic Plane Crashes In Paris

JUNE 3

TRAGEDY HIT THE PARIS AIR Show today when the second prototype of the Soviet Union's *Tupolev Tu-144* supersonic airliner exploded during a demonstration flight (pictured), killing its crew of six. The *Tu-144* was the world's first commercial supersonic airliner but, unlike the Anglo-French *Concorde,* which it resembled, it would not prove a success in the long term.

Its loss was a major blow to Soviet civil aviation plans, and though the type would be introduced into freight service by Aeroflot in 1975 and passenger flights would begin two years later, it was withdrawn in 1978 after just 102 operational flights. It was believed another fatal crash occurred during a test flight.

ARRIVALS

Born this month:
25: Jamie Redknapp, UK football player

DEPARTURES

Died this month:
10: William Inge, American playwright (*Come Back Little Sheba, Picnic, Bus Stop, Spendor In The Grass,* etc), aged 60
26: John Cranko, British dancer, choreographer, aged 45

JUNE 30

US Bombs Stop But Cambodia's Grief Continues

The last days of June witnessed renewed fighting in Cambodia when communist rebels launched a major offensive on the country's capital, Phnom Penh. Today, they were reported to be in control of Highway 4, the only supply route from the crucial port of Kompong Sum.

In Washington, Congress had prevented further US bombing of Cambodia, cutting off funds at the end of May, to the dismay of President Nixon who feared that the country would fall to the communists without US air support.

JUNE 24

Russian Summit In Washington

Improved East-West relations were very much in evidence today as Soviet premier Leonid Brezhnev concluded a nine-day official state visit to the US. The Russian leader was the unlikely guest of honour at a 'pool party' in Los Angeles, where he rubbed shoulders with Hollywood glitterati.

President Richard Nixon, grateful for the diversion from Watergate revelations, spent the week in private discussions with Brezhnev who, as he was leaving, remarked with characteristic brevity that the trip had left him with a 'good feeling'. Whether this was due to the Hollywood reception, or the furthering of Soviet-US relations, was unclear.

The Name's Moore – Roger Moore

A new James Bond was strutting his stuff on the screen this month. George Lazenby had filled the breach for a single film after Sean Connery's decision to step down as Ian Fleming's secret agent, but Roger Moore – formerly known for his portrayal of TV's long-running *The Saint* – was making *Live And Let Die* (pictured with Jane Seymour) the movie blockbuster of the year. Moore, 44, had made his Hollywood début as long ago as 1954, in *The Last Time I Saw Paris,* but was better known for UK TV roles such as the Leslie Charteris hero which proved the prototype for Bond. Meanwhile, thanks to the distinctively English combination of Moore and Paul McCartney, who provided the essential Bond signature tune, *Live And Let Die* proved there was indeed life after Connery for 007!

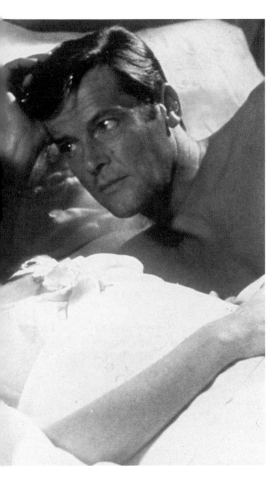

Watergate – Dean Says Nixon Knew Of Cover-Up

THE SENATE WATERGATE hearings in Washington were hit by the most dramatic turn yet today when President Nixon's former counsel, John Dean, said that the President had known about, and taken part in, the illegal cover-up of White House involvement in the Watergate burglary for eight months.

Accusing former Nixon aides John Ehrlichman and 'Bob' Haldeman of organizing the cover-up, Dean claimed he had told Nixon that the effort to hide White House involvement - and other acts - was 'a cancer growing on the presidency'.

Dean's statements were the most damning yet heard by the Senate committee. According to Dean, not only was the President actively involved in impeding justice, he had also suggested it would be easy to find $1 million in 'hush money', and had tried to implicate others - including former Attorney-General John Mitchell - in a bid to find a fall-guy.

Clearly nervous and upset, Dean left the hearing refusing to talk to waiting press and TV journalists eager to pump him for further details.

SPORT

SIMPSON TURNS ON THE JUICE TO GAIN SUPERSTARDOM

The immense amount of hours and column inches devoted by the US media to the trial, for his wife's murder, of former football player OJ Simpson in 1994-95 puzzled many outside the US.

Alright, so he was a TV celebrity and some-time relatively small-time film actor, and he had been a successful athlete in a very popular and heavily-hyped game. But he'd retired from that in 1979, for heaven's sake! What was the big deal?

The answer to that lies in events this year, when Orenthal James Simpson, star running back with the Buffalo Bills, ran himself into the history books - and the consciousness of a nation hungry for new heroes - when he smashed the NFL rushing record for a season with 2003 yards. That put him in the same company as the legendary Jim Brown, the early-1960s Cleveland Browns star whose record of 1863 yards Simpson demolished.

Unlike Brown, who'd been a prickly, taciturn, even surly character, OJ Simpson was approachable, voluble and articulate, very good looking and already had a formidable record on which he was building. He'd first earned headlines in 1967 when, playing for the University of Southern California (USC) against local rivals, the University of California Los Angeles (UCLA), Simpson made an electrifying and game-winning 64-yard touchdown run which is still held as one of the greatest in American Football.

A gifted athlete, Simpson had also been a member of the USC relay team which set a new world record for the 4 x 100 yds, and had personal best time for the 100 yds of 9.4 seconds. But it was on the football ground that Simpson shone brightest and, after winning the 1969 Heisman Memorial Trophy as the year's best college player, he was drafted by the Buffalo Bills.

For two seasons he performed only adequately, but a new head coach rectified that by making Simpson the key to the Bills' offense. The rewards? This year's record-breaking figures and a career total - until 1977 with the Bills, and for a final two years with the San Francisco 49ers - of 11,236 yards and 61 touchdowns.

Even now, with a 30-year gap looming between his retirement and the present, OJ Simpson remains in the top five all-time great rushers, his post-retirement career as a sports commentator, talk-show guest and capable actor ensuring that he remained a hero.

Hence all the fuss surrounding that California court-room.

RED RUM STARTS RECORD NATIONAL FEAT

A modern British horse-racing legend began at Liverpool's Aintree racecourse this March when Red Rum won the first of his eventual record-breaking three Grand National steeplechases - an achievement which was only enhanced by the fact that in between his second win, in 1974, and his third, in 1977, Red Rum scored two second places in a formidable race a high percentage of entrants never even finish.

Aged just eight this year, when he gave away 21 lbs to the second-placed Crisp, the champion would prove himself a National Hunt wizard, winning 24 of his 100 races between 1967-78 for a prize record of £145,234 (about $300,000), as well as three out of ten flat races.

By the time he won his third Grand National, when his dawn training sessions on the sands of Southport attracted huge crowds, Red Rum was a genuine superstar – a status confirmed in 1988 when a life-sized statue of him was unveiled at Aintree.

'BIG-MOUTH' CLOUGH QUITS DERBY

No stranger to controversy, English soccer manager Brian Clough made headlines again this year when he and his assistant, Peter Taylor, walked out of Derby County, the team they'd taken to the 1971-72 League title, after a row with chairman Sam Longson.

He disapproved of Clough's high-profile comments on other teams and players in the media, a view which appeared justified with the furore which later greeted Clough's televised remarks prior to England's World Cup qualifying game against Poland at Wembley.

Never a man prone to understatement, Clough mockingly described Poland's goalkeeper, Jan Tomaszewski, as 'a clown'. Inevitably, that clown broke the home supporters' hearts by restricting England to just one goal. The resulting 1-1 draw confirmed Poland's right to go to the 1974 World Cup Finals in West Germany, and England's failure to qualify for the first time.

Brian Clough - never a man prone to understatement

Farewell To Betty, US Forces Sweetheart

MILLIONS OF AMERICAN VETERANS of World War II were stunned today to hear that Betty Grable, the undisputed glamour queen of 1940s Hollywood, had died at the age of 56. Grable was practically born performing, studying ballet and tap from an early age and starting work on a chorus line on Broadway at the tender age of 13. But it was in her mid-20s, having made the move into films, that she gained widespread popularity, especially among US troops serving far from home.

As their number-one pin-up, with legs that were reputedly insured with Lloyds of London for $1 million, she graced many a servicemen's locker, and found film fame starring in the likes of *Down Argentine Way* (1940), *Coney Island* (1943), *Pin-Up Girl* (1944) and *The Dolly Sisters* (1945).

Grable's biggest hit, the 1953 film *How To Marry A Millionaire* found her teamed up with fellow sex symbols Lauren Bacall and Marilyn Monroe. And, just as Monroe was commemorated by Elton John's *Candle In the Wind,* so US singer-songwriter Neil Sedaka would be inspired to pen his own tribute, *Betty Grable.*

JULY 10

Bahamas Gain Independence

Prince Charles was present in Nassau, capital of the Bahamas, today to hand over the documents conferring sovereignty to the country's first black Prime Minister, Lynden Oscar Pindling. The group of over 700 islands was now independent of British rule after 300 years.

Already a centre for tourism, the new Prime Minister planned to raise his country's profile in the banking world, allowing it to become a centre for off-shore funds. This aim would not have been helped by the fact that many of the white population had sold up and moved off the islands, feeling that the move to independence would cause political instability.

JULY 7

Tennis Stars Boycott Wimbledon

Top tennis professionals today announced their intention of boycotting this year's Wimbledon Championships, in protest at contracts offered them by the sport's governing body, the Lawn Tennis Federation. The boycott, by members of the Association of Tennis Professionals meant that 13 of the 16 top-seeded men players would not be gracing the famous Centre Court – or any other Wimbledon court – this year.

The result was an unexpected win for Czechoslovakian Jan Kodes, promoted to second seed. He beat Russia's first ever Wimbledon finalist, Alex Metreveli, in three sets - 6-1, 9-8, 6-3. Romanian rebel Ilie Nastase, the pre-tournament favourite and first seed, failed to make the final. As expected, Billie-Jean retained her Ladies Singles title by beating fellow American Chris Evert.

UK TOP 10 SINGLES

1: Welcome Home
- Peters & Lee
2: Skweeze Me Pleeze Me
- Slade
3: Life On Mars
- David Bowie
4: Born To Be With You
- Dave Edmunds
5: Snoopy Vs The Red Baron
- Hotshots
6: Take Me To The Mardi Gras
- Paul Simon
7: Rubber Bullets
- 10cc
8: Saturday Night's Alright For Fighting
- Elton John
9: I'm The Leader Of The Gang (I Am)
- Gary Glitter
10: Albatross
- Fleetwood Mac

JULY 9

Amin Expels Peace Corps From Uganda

In the latest of a series of unexpected and irrational moves against foreigners, President Idi Amin (pictured) of Uganda today ordered the arrest and expulsion of 112 workers from the American Peace Corps, setting himself on a collision course with the United States.

Established in 1961, the Peace Corps was set up by President John F Kennedy as America's response to requests for help from third-world countries. Since then, Corps volunteers – many of them young graduates – had taught basic skills in nutrition, engineering and agriculture throughout the world.

The latest turn of events followed a row earlier in the month when the US banned the Ugandan Ambassador after Amin insulted President Nixon over the Watergate affair.

JULY 17

Oval Office Bugged, Says Aide

SENATE INVESTIGATORS into the Watergate cover-up couldn't believe their luck today when a White House official revealed to their hearing that not only was the Nixon administration capable of illegally wiretapping the opposition, but had possibly sealed its own fate by bugging the Oval Office itself!

The latest stunning development in the saga fast unfolding in Washington came during the testimony of Alexander Butterfield, a middle-level White House aide in charge of routine administration. He revealed that listening devices had been installed in the Oval Office and other rooms, and on telephones used by President Nixon, with taped recordings stored away for future use.

According to Butterfield, all the devices were still in place, and still in use. The Senate committee were quick to realize that those tapes, if they could be heard, would provide conclusive evidence of the President's innocence – or guilt.

Two days later, President Nixon set himself on what would prove a fatal collision course with the committee, and the American people, when he said he would not hand the tapes over to Senate investigators.

JULY 30

Thalidomide Victims Win Payout

In Britain, an 11-year fight by victims of the drug thalidomide was finally settled today, with compensation awards totalling £20 million ($50m). Thalidomide was used in the late 1950s and early 1960s to combat morning sickness in pregnant women, but was found to cause grave deformities in the babies to which they gave birth – usually short and relatively useless limbs.

The drug, which was never granted a licence in the United States, was nevertheless marketed heavily in Britain and West Germany. Upwards of 10,000 babies were born deformed or dead to mothers who had been given it.

Distillers (UK), the company whose pharmaceuticals division marketed thalidomide in Britain, had found its alcohol products withdrawn from major food chainstores earlier this year as public opinion massed behind the victims in their fight for compensation. A row would break out when it was discovered that trust funds set up were liable for UK tax, and it was not until October 1974 that the British Government set aside £5 million to offset the tax liability.

Getty's Grandson Kidnapped

Teenager Paul Getty III (pictured), the grandson of billionaire Paul Getty, was kidnapped in Rome today. His Italian kidnappers announced that they were asking for a ransom of $750,000 to secure his safe release.

The young man would have to endure six months of captivity, during which time the kidnappers cut off his ear and sent it to his family as an incentive to pay. He was eventually released on December 14.

Kidnapping was something of an industry among the world's criminal classes in the 1970s, British businessman Charles Lockwood, kidnapped in Argentina last month, was not the only foreign national to be snatched in that country.

Later in the year, a $10 million ransom was paid by Exxon, the US oil company, for the release of its executive Victor Samuelson, who disappeared from their Buenos Aires refinery.

JULY

Fifty Killed In Isle Of Man Holiday Disaster

THE FULL EXTENT OF THE HORROR which hit the Isle of Man yesterday was reinforced by today's official confirmation that as many as 50 people had died in the wake of the devastating fire which ripped through the £2 million Summerland holiday complex in the capital, Douglas.

The vast entertainment complex - said to be the world's largest - which incorporated a funfair, disco, solarium, restaurants and theatre, caught alight at the height of the summer season when it was packed with hundreds of holidaymakers.

The blaze, which also accounted for almost 100 serious burns and other injuries, was so large and so fierce that all the island's firefighting resources were called to the scene.

Not all the deaths were a result of the fire itself, which spread rapidly. Many were crushed in the stampede to get out of the burning building, and survivors reported that some people had been forced to kick their way through windows to escape the flames.

AUGUST 13

Bank Robber Alleges MI6 Dublin Bomb Plot

British Defence Minister Lord Carrington today refused to comment on allegations made on Irish television that MI6, the UK's senior secret service department, was responsible for planting a number of bombs in central Dublin - a plot which had led to the Republic's government introducing stringent anti-IRA laws.

The charges were made by Kenneth Littlejohn, a Briton sentenced to 20 years in prison for his part in a Dublin bank robbery. He claimed that he had been employed by MI6, whose plan was to stir up antagonism to the IRA with explosive devices manufactured in indentical style to those constructed by the Republican extremists.

Lord Carrington's silence came in the face of Ulster MPs' demands for an inquiry into British intelligence operations in the Irish Republic.

AUGUST 6

Stevie's Wonder-ful Recovery From Crash

Motown soul star Stevie Wonder, 23, suffered severe head injuries today near Salisbury, North Carolina, when the car in which he was a passenger collided with a truck carrying logs. Rushed to hospital, he would remain in a coma for four days.

Thankfully, the multi-talented Stevie would recover, apart from permanent loss of his sense of smell. Physicians said that the impact of the accident was three times worse for the blind singer than it would have been for a sighted person as he had not been able to prepare himself for the impact.

Balderstone Loses Battle Of The Balls

Chris Balderstone, one of the dwindling band of British summer-and-winter sportsmen who combined professional careers in football and cricket, was stripped of the captaincy of Carlisle United FC this month after deciding to continue playing county cricket until the end of the season instead of returning for duty at his football team's Brunton Park ground.

Balderstone, 32, clearly thought that his career as a cricketer was more likely to provide longevity and security than the alternative. He missed Carlisle's first games but, despite this setback, continued to play League football for the Cumbrian team and, in 1975, Doncaster Rovers.

UK TOP 10 SINGLES

1: I'm The Leader Of The Gang (I Am)
- Garry Glitter

2: Welcome Home
- Peters & Lee

3: Yesterday Once More
- The Carpenters

4: 49 Crash
- Suzie Quatro

5: Alright Alright Alright
- Mungo Jerry

6: Spanish Eyes
- Al Martino

7: Going Home
- The Osmonds

8: You Can Do Magic
- Limmie & The Family Cookin'

9: Life On Mars
- David Bowie

10: Touch Me In The Morning
- Diana Ross

ARRIVALS

Born this month:
14: Kieren Perkins, Australian, Commonwealth, World and Olympic swimming champion

DEPARTURES

Died this month:
1: Walter Ulbricht, East German politician, aged 80 *(see Came & Went pages)*
4: Eddie Condon, American jazz guitarist, aged 67
6: Fulgencio Batistá, Cuban dictator overthrown by Fidel Castro, died in exile, aged 72
7: Freddie Cox, former Spurs and Arsenal soccer player, aged 52 ;
Jack Gregory, Australian fast bowler, 24 Test matches 1919-29
9: Steve Perron, US singer with The Children and occasional writer for Texan band ZZ Top, aged 28.
17: Paul Williams, American singer (The Temptations), aged 34
31: John Ford, US Academy Award winning film director *(see main story)*

AUGUST 8

US Vice-President In Bribery Scandal

Just when it didn't seem possible that a beleaguered White House could cope with any more scandal, Vice-President Spiro T Agnew (pictured) today admitted that he was being investigated for alleged extortion and bribery of contractors during his time as Governor of Maryland and, previously, as County Executive in Baltimore.

Despite shrugging off the charges as 'damned lies', Agnew must have known that the Baltimore federal grand jury was likely to uncover uncomfortable facts, though it was likely that he, like President Nixon, believed his very position would safeguard his future. As it would transpire, Agnew's confidence was ill-judged.

Cod War Reaches Fatal Peak

BETWEEN 1972 AND 1976 a running 'battle of wits' took place in the North Atlantic between Britain and Iceland in what became known as the Icelandic Cod War. The dispute between the two countries over fishing limits eventually deteriorated to the point where both countries' fishing fleets needed the protection of their respective navies.

In May, a British Royal Navy gunboat had chased an Icelandic frigate in what was the first officially sanctioned action. Reaction in Iceland was prompt and deeply felt – the British Embassy in Reykjavík was surrounded by angry Icelanders protesting at Britain's action.

Today saw the first fatality of the Cod War. An engineer on an Icelandic gunboat was killed when his vessel collided with a Royal Navy ship. Tragedy would turn to farce in September when, while recriminations and accusations over this incident still flew between London and Reykjavík, the crew of a Royal Navy frigate were accused of throwing carrots at another Icelandic gunboat!

Ford, Hollywood's Favourite Irishman, Dies

Hollywood lost one of its most flamboyant, gifted and decorated directors today with the death, at the age of 78, of the legendary John Ford.

Ford, whose career in the movies began in the early years of the century, died at his home in Palm Springs, California. Known as 'Pappy' to the actors who worked for him during his long and distinguished career, the notoriously hard-drinking Ford was born in Maine, christened Sean Aloysius O'Feeney and was raised in Ireland before joining his brother in Hollywood at the age of eighteen.

Early directorial successes, including the classics *Stagecoach* and *Young Mr Lincoln,* secured Ford the position as head of the OSS propaganda film unit during World War II, where he made documentaries such as *The Battle Of Midway* in 1942. In all he won five Academy Awards - for *The Informer, The Grapes Of Wrath, How Green Was My Valley, The Quiet Man,* and *The Battle Of Midway* – more than any other director in history.

Malibu Marriage For Kristoffersons

Singers Kris Kristofferson and Rita Coolidge were married in Malibu, California today. Coolidge, a fast-rising solo star, wore traditional white for the ceremony. It was a second marriage for Kristofferson, a former Rhodes scholar and Oxford University student whose songs *Me And Bobby McGee* and *Help Me Make It Through The Night* had become modern standards. The couple would be on the road together constantly for the next six years, recording two albums, before their professional and personal partnership ended in 1979.

Donny And The Osmonds - The Family That Played Together

Hard though it may be to believe, The Osmonds had been household names in the US for almost ten years before their outstanding domestic success suddenly leaped the Atlantic and they became - with no exaggeration - the single most consistent pop act between 1972 and 1976 in terms of chart performance and sales.

It was in 1962 that The Osmond Brothers - Alan, Wayne, Merrill and Jay - were signed to appear as regular guests on the top-rated *Andy Williams Show* for what would eventually prove to be a five-year stay. Becoming The Osmonds soon after, they were joined in 1963 by their six-year-old brother, Donny, to become one of America's favourite TV acts.

That was built on when the Williams show ended, when they switched with equal impact in 1969, to a regular guest slot on the *Jerry Lewis Show*. In 1971, with The Jackson Five starting to create waves, MGM Records boss Mike Curb signed The Osmonds to a recording contract. The rest, as they say, became history.

Through 1971, the group scored hits with two albums and two big singles - their début *One Bad Apple* (a US No 1 for five weeks) and *Yo-Yo* (a US No 3), while Donny Osmond's first two solo releases (*Sweet And Innocent* and *Go Away Little Girl*) were both US Top 10 million-sellers, as were the two albums on which they featured.

The roll had continued through 1972, when the group's next US hit single, *Down By The Lazy River*, also became their first British hit while Donny was hitting the US No 3 spot (and selling another million) with his version of the oldie *Puppy Love*. When released in Britain in June, it would race to No 1 and re-enter the charts on no less than three later occasions.

In May, Donny's third solo LP, *Portrait Of Donny*, had reached No 6 in the US, and in June The Osmonds' nine-year-old brother, Jimmy, had joined the gravy train to release *Long Haired Lover From Liverpool*. Not an especially big hit in the US, by year end it would spend five weeks at the top of the UK charts, sell nearly a million and give the chubby little chap the distinction of being the youngest-ever UK chart-topper in history.

In September, a cartoon series, *The Osmonds,* began transmission in Britain to add fuel to the teen fire, which climaxed in December when the group hit No 2 (behind Jimmy) with *Crazy Horses* and Donny notched into No 3 with *Why*.

That's how it stood when this year opened, with the added bonus of Donny's new album, *Too Young,* at No 7 in the UK chart. By April, he was No 1 again in the UK singles chart with *The 12th Of Never* and at No 8 in the US. Jimmy had also returned, with his *Tweedle Dee,* the UK No 4 single.

In May, Donny's LP *Alone Together* was No 6 in the UK and No 36 in the US, while July saw The Osmonds back in the UK singles chart, at No 4, with *Going Home,* a track from the concept album about their Mormon faith, *The Plan*. That would be the UK's No 6 best-selling album in August.

September saw Donny back at the UK No 1 spot with *Young Love* and, just when we all thought the Osmond family had no more tricks up its sleeves, in November the 14-year-old Marie Osmond scored her first hit with *Paper*

Roses. By mid-December that was Britain's No 2 single, with Donny's *When I Fall In Love* perched at No 4.

Donny, The Osmonds, Marie and the teaming of Donny and Marie would continue to rack up hits until the end of 1975 when things began to slow and the older brothers began to peel off to work on solo projects. Marie became one of America's most successful country singers, and Donny began dividing his time between a Las Vegas career and building a family with his wife.

In the early 1980s he'd score a few middling comeback hits, but would see in the 1990s as a stage musical star. Four of Alan's eight offspring would be launched as The Osmond Brothers in the early 1990s. And Little Jimmy? He'd grow up to head a TV production and tour management company which was closely involved with Michael Jackson's Bad world tour and be responsible for much of Prince's early live work.

The Osmonds

QUEEN - THE EARLY DAYS

Days of international superstardom, sell-out world tours, multi-platinum albums and the rest were still a wild dream for Queen - Freddie Mercury, Brian May, John Deacon and Roger Taylor - as 1973 dawned.

Signed to a recording deal with EMI only two months earlier, they and producers Roy Thomas Baker and John Anthony were still putting the finishing touches to their début album (to be called *Queen* - what else?) at Trident Studios in London and rehearsing madly for the launch gig they knew EMI had planned at the legendary Marquee Club on April 9. That went well, and media response was positive.

To fill in time, and for a laugh, Freddie Mercury recorded a new version of the oldie *I Can Hear Music* under the name Larry Lurex. Thankfully for Queen's future, Larry Lurex didn't click with the record-buying public - but, to everyone's surprise, neither did the *Queen* album, nor their first single, *Keep Yourself Alive.*

While this flop would have defeated most bands, Queen were made of sterner stuff. They began work on a second album for release in 1975 and accepted Mott The Hoople lead singer Ian Hunter's offer of a support spot on a forthcoming UK tour, due to start in November.

SEPT

Chile's Allende Killed In CIA-Backed Coup

CONFUSION SURROUNDED THE DEATH today of President Salvador Allende (pictured) of Chile during a right-wing military coup described by its leader, General Augusto Pinochet, as being designed 'to free the country from the Marxist yoke'. Although the US administration would strenuously deny widespread accusations that the CIA had played an active role in the coup, it would later be learned that this had, in fact, been the case.

First reports from the presidential palace, which was bombarded by rockets and bombs, seemed to suggest that Allende had committed suicide. Others claimed he was shot defending the palace, but later reports said that his widow believed he was assassinated.

The world's first democratically elected Marxist leader, President Allende had, on gaining office in 1970, promised to convert Chile to socialism within a democratic framework. However, mounting opposition from the affluent middle classes and the military eventually cost him his ambitious vision and his life.

Allende's socialist policies had led to the seizure of assets belonging to American companies in Chile, while the US was known to have been hostile to the government in power. The CIA had fomented unrest by underwriting a nationwide strike by the powerful National Confederation of Lorry Owners which effectively made Chilean society, already hit by other industrial chaos, grind to a halt.

Chile's new government was to be led by General Pinochet and, within a week, it announced the court-martial of over 5,000 civilians in what was seen as a purge of left-wing supporters and sympathizers.

SEPTEMBER 3

Kissinger Is New US Secretary Of State

Henry Kissinger, the 50-year-old German-American political academic-turned-mediator, was appointed President Nixon's Secretary of State today, succeeding the resigning William Rogers.

The US President's Special Adviser on National Security since 1969, the former Harvard Professor of Government had acted as Nixon's wandering semi-official ambassador in trips to China and the Soviet Union, and had been the principal US negotiator in the Paris talks which appeared to have secured peace in Vietnam.

Kissinger, who was born in Fürth, Germany, would share this year's Nobel Peace Prize with North Vietnam's Le Duc Tho for that achievement - an award his opposite number would decline.

SEPTEMBER 2

Farewell To Tolkien, Lord of the Rings

British academic and novelist John Ronald Reuel (JRR) Tolkien, creator of *Lord Of The Rings* and *The Hobbit*, died today in Oxford – but did so in the knowledge that Middle Earth - the fantasy world which he had created, and for which he had developed several complete languages - would endure as classics of literature.

Born in 1892, Tolkien, an academic philologist, initially created the characters which peopled *The Hobbit* to entertain his children, and did not publish the story in book form until 1937. That, and the complex *Lord Of The Rings* trilogy which followed (*The Fellowship Of The Ring, The Two Towers* and *The Return Of The King*), was considered *avant garde* when it first appeared, but they all inspired a plethora of sword and sorcery-style imitations, as well as crossing over into rock music, cinema and television in the 1960s and '70s when rediscovered by the 'flower power' generation.

SEPTEMBER 17

Equal Opportunities For UK Women

Today saw the first official mention of a body which was to exert a powerful influence on employment matters in Britain for many years to come. The Equal Opportunities Commission was one suggestion contained in a government report entitled Equal Opportunities for Men and Women which Home Secretary Robert Carr hoped would lay the groundwork for women's rights in the workplace. This would be the first time that equality in employment for both men and women would be guaranteed under British law.

SEPTEMBER 7

World Racing Champ Jackie Stewart Retires

VISIBLY UPSET BY THE DEATH of his Tyrrell-Ford team-mate, François Cevert, during a practice for the US Grand Prix at Watkins Glen, New York, Formula One's most successful driver - Scotsman Jackie Stewart (pictured) - announced that he would not take part in the race and was quitting the sport.

Over the past few years Stewart, who was already assured of retaining his world championship when he made his shock announcement, had been deeply concerned with safety standards in motor-racing. The fact that he pulled out just before his 100th Grand Prix race indicated that – despite being at the very peak of his career – he felt very strongly that the risks were no longer worth taking.

Stewart would continue his association with motor racing as a commentator, his record of 27 Grand Prix victories in eight years making his contributions invaluable.

SEPT

SEPTEMBER 20

Billie-Jean Triumphs In Battle Of Sexes

Billie Jean King, who won a record number of Wimbledon tennis titles, will probably not be best be remembered for her resounding defeat today of fellow American player Bobby Riggs.

Riggs, who could - in all truth - be described as the greatest male chauvinist to ever set foot on a tennis court, had unwisely claimed that women's tennis was of little consequence and that no woman could hope to beat him on court.

Unfortunately, Riggs had his bluff well and truly called by Mrs King, who succeeded in beating him in their much-publicized 'Battle of the Sexes' at the Houston Astrodome in Texas. The 55-year-old Riggs lost 6-4, 6-3, 6-3 in front of a nationwide TV audience of 50 million.

SEPTEMBER 28

Anglo-American Auden Closes Book

Poet, playwright and critic WH Auden died today, aged 66, at his summer home in Kirchstetten, near Vienna. Widely accepted as one of the most gifted poets of the twentieth century, Auden was born in York, studied at Oxford in the 1920s and became a leading member of the influential, left-wing 'Pylon Poets' – Stephen Spender, C Day Lewis, Christopher Isherwood and Louis MacNeice – so-called for their poetic use of industrial imagery: pylons, factories, roads and trains. His first volume of poetry, which appeared in 1930, was entitled simply *Poems* and established him as one of the major voices of his generation. Emigrating to the US in 1939, at the end of a period which he famously described as 'that low, dishonest decade', Auden became an American citizen in 1946.

Continuing to write prolifically, Auden did not sever his British ties, becoming Professor of Poetry at Oxford between 1956 and 1961 and eventually returning to his old college, Christ Church, in the early 1970s.

SEPTEMBER 21

Pollock Painting Tops $2 Million

A new American auction record for a contemporary painting was set in New York today when an abstract by US artist Jackson Pollock fetched a cool $2 million. Pollock's style was not to everyone's taste, yet attracted wide acclaim from critics who saw deep meaning in what his detractors viewed as aimless dollops, streaks and coarsely-mixed textures.

The artist himself would not benefit from the millions his painting cost the successful bidder. He had died in a car crash in 1956, aged only 44.

OCT

No Peace For Yom Kippur
As Israel Repels Arab Armies

THE PEACE OF THE SACRED Jewish holiday of Yom Kippur was shattered today when Egyptian forces launched a surprise attack on Israel, crossing the Suez Canal and taking control of the East Bank. At the same time, the strategically-important Golan Heights were invaded by Syrian troops, who advanced 15 miles into Israeli-occupied territory.

Israel had steadfastly refused to negotiate the return of territories occupied since the 1967 Six-Day War and Arab patience had finally run out. Iraq, Jordan and Libya also provided support to the attack, which met with ferocious Israeli resistance. During the course of the war, which would last nearly a month, Israel retook the Golan

Heights and began pushing Syrian forces back towards Damascus, where an Israeli bombing raid caused widespread loss of lives among the civilian population.

Despite the destruction of nine bridges across the Suez Canal, Egyptian forces on the East Bank engaged the Israelis in one of the most violent tank battles ever fought.

At the height of the conflict, on October 26, President Nixon ordered US troops to full alert worldwide. Intelligence reports suggested the Soviet Union intended to take an active role in support of the Arab nations, but a stand-down was ordered once the White House received pledges of non-intervention from Soviet leader Leonid Brezhnev.

King Of Rock Reigns Alone

Given the wall of secrecy which surrounded his private life, Elvis Presley's millions of fans around the world were stunned today when they learned that Elvis and Priscilla Presley had been granted a divorce in a Santa Monica, California, courthouse. The news spelled the official end of a rock'n'roll love affair that had started when Sergeant 53310761 Presley, E was posted to Germany for his national service in the late 1950s. The couple had met in September 1959, in Bad Neuheim, where the 14-year-old Priscilla Beaulieu - as she then was - lived with her mother and stepfather, a US Air Force captain. Their friendship deepened and, when Elvis was discharged from the Army in 1960, Priscilla moved into his Graceland mansion in Memphis - rigorously chaperoned, it was said, by one of Presley's aunts. The couple finally married in 1967, in Las Vegas. Elvis and Priscilla would remain in contact through their daughter, Lisa Marie, who would herself marry a pop icon - Michael Jackson - in May 1994. In fact, once initial tensions between them faded, the two would remain friends until Presley's death in August 1977.

South African Apartheid Intensifies

New laws came into force in South Africa forbidding the mixing of different races in private social gatherings. The policy of apartheid, meaning 'separation', had been part and parcel of South African law since 1948 when the National Party came to power.

This latest addition to the apartheid laws, which aimed to enforce racial segregation and promote white supremacy, came at a time when international opposition to the policy was increasing.

UK Radio Airwaves Go Independent

Many had tried – and few succeeded – to break the state monopoly of broadcasting in Britain. The most notable effort was made by Radio Caroline, whose broadcasting from the vessel Mi Amigo moored outside British territorial waters, successfully survived into the 1980s.

From today, however, the BBC faced competition from the country's first legal mainland commercial radio station. It came in the form of LBC (the London Broadcasting Company), which would transmit current affairs and news programmes.

It was to be followed the next day by Capital Radio, which was to provide Londoners with an alternative diet of music and light entertainment similar to the state-owned Radio 1.

UK TOP 10 SINGLES

1: Eye Level
- The Simon Park Orchestra
2: My Friend Stan
- Slade
3: Nutbush City Limits
- Ike and Tina Turner
4: Ballroom Blitz
- Sweet
5: Monster Mash
- Bobby 'Boris' Pickett & The Crypt Kickers
6: The Laughing Gnome
- David Bowie
7: For The Good Times
- Perry Como
8: Daydreamer/The Puppy Song
- David Cassidy
9: Caroline
- Status Quo
10: Goodbye Yellow Brick Road
- Elton John

ARRIVALS
Born this month:
16: David Unsworth, UK football player

DEPARTURES
Died this month:
2: Paavo Nurmi, Finnish superstar athlete ('The Flying Finn'), winner of 9 Olympic gold medals (1500m and 5000m in 1924, 10,000m in 1920 and 1928, 3000m steeplechase in 1924, cross-country team and individual in 1920 and 1924), carried the Olympic torch to open 1952 Helsinki Games, aged 76
16: Gene Krupa, American jazz drummer, aged 64
22: Pablo Casals, Spanish classical cellist and conductor, aged 96
25: Abebe Bikila, Ethiopian Olympic marathon champion, 1960, 1964
26: Sir Roger Henry Hollis, British security chief, aged 67

OCTOBER 12

Sleaze Buries Agnew - Ford Is VP As Nixon Turns Tapes In

EVENTS IN WASHINGTON hit a new downward spiral this month as a fresh sleaze scandal forced the resignation of President Nixon's deputy, Spiro T Agnew, the arrival of a new, unelected Vice President, and the firing of the Watergate prosecutor by a President forced into the humiliating U-turn of handing over the secret White House tapes he must have known spelled the end of his bluff and his political career.

The first disaster to strike the Nixon camp came on October 12, when Vice President Agnew resigned after agreeing not to contest a Federal charge of tax evasion and bribery while Governor of Maryland. By doing this, Agnew escaped a possible prison sentence for failing to declare $29,500 of income. Instead, he was merely fined $10,000 and given three years' probation.

His replacement was Gerald Ford, the Republican leader in the House of Representatives and therefore - according to the US Constitution - the legal successor to the Vice President. Although Ford's appointment had to be ratified by both houses of Congress, the moderate minority leader got the expected unanimous nod - though few could have dreamed that they were, in fact, approving the appointment of a man who would ascend to the White House when a disgraced Nixon finally bowed to the inevitable and became the first US President ever to resign.

Nixon's actions helped make that inevitable when, on October 23, he reluctantly agreed to Watergate prosecutor Archibald Cox's order to hand the White House tapes over to Judge Sirica - but not before he had managed to persuade Solicitor-General Robert Bork to sack Cox.

Bork had only agreed after Attorney-General Elliot Richardson and his deputy, William Ruckelshaus, had both refused to do so, and then resigned. Richard Nixon had only succeeded in digging himself deeper into the mire.

OCTOBER 31

IRA Men Escape Jail In Helicopter

IRA terrorists used a hijacked helicopter to stage a daring jail-break near Dublin today, when they landed in a prison exercise yard to lift three colleagues to freedom. Among the three whisked from Mountjoy Prison was Seamus Twomey, regarded as one of the most dangerous IRA leaders to operate in Ulster. He was serving a three-year sentence for IRA membership - illegal in the Irish Republic - and receiving stolen money.

Brave Banks Calls It A Day After Losing Eye

The glittering career of Stoke City's England international goalkeeper Gordon Banks was officially confirmed as ended today, a year after he lost one of his eyes in a car crash as he drove home after attending the club's Victoria Ground for routine treatment. Such was Banks' stature - he was one of the English team that won the 1966 World Cup - that British TV programmes were interrupted with reports on his progress in hospital as surgeons fought, unsuccessfully, to save his left eye. Banks would never play competitive football again, but bowed out at the top after 251 appearances in the Stoke goal. One of his last games had been in the club's historic League Cup win against Chelsea at the end of the 1972 season – their first major prize in an 84-year history. He also won 73 England caps and was rated as one of the world's most outstanding goalkeepers of all time.

OCT

films like *Enter The Dragon*, released later this year, fuelled his legend.

It was Lee's third Hong Kong-made film (he'd starred in *Fist Of Fury* and *The Big Boss* in 1972, while he also had *The Way Of The Dragon* completed and ready for release as a sequel to *Enter The Dragon*), following a bit part in the 1969 Hollywood production *Marlowe* and a stab at a supporting role in the US television series *The Green Hornet*.

Lee provided Western cinema-goers with a prototype action hero, long before the advent of Stallone and Schwarzenegger, and a Kung Fu craze swept Europe and the United States in the form of films, magazines and even records - Carl Douglas's *Kung Fu Fighting* was a UK chart-topper and a major US hit in 1974.

Yet exiled Chinese felt ambivalent about a man who offered a crudely stereotyped image and, in one critic's words, represented, 'a strident symbol of their own compromised identity'. Lee's son, Brandon - also an action film star - died during the making of *The Crow* in 1994, his posthumous fame and the film's relative success providing a bizarre echo of his father's end.

JULY 19
BRUCE LEE - ETERNAL KING OF KUNG FU

The cult of the Kung Fu movie was dealt a severe blow today by the demise of Bruce Lee, martial arts expert and the single most successful star of the genre, in Hong Kong.

Aged only 32, Lee's official cause of death was acute cerebral oedema - a brain haemorrhage - yet the San Franciscan son of a Cantonese opera star would live on as

JANUARY 26
EDWARD G. ROBINSON - MASTER OF MENACE

One of Hollywood's most reliable and potent actors for 50 years, no-one (with the possible exception of Humphrey Bogart or James Cagney) played a tough guy with such quiet and menacing confidence as Edward G. Robinson, who died today in Hollywood after a long illness, at the age of 76.

Born Emanuel Goldenberg and of Romanian extraction, Robinson began his acting career on the New York stage in 1913, but by 1923 had been coaxed to the West Coast to begin making the first of almost 90 films. It was the seventh of those - the 1930 classic gangster movie *Little Caesar* - which made him a star. It was a status he would never lose, even though he would appear in his fair share of turkeys. Definitely not turkeys, and the reason why Robinson remained a firm box-office favourite, were such great films as *The Whole Town's Talking* (1934), the original version of *Kid Galahad* (1937), *A Slight Case Of Murder* (1938), the chilling *Double Indemnity* and *The Woman In The Window* (both 1944), as well as his two 1948 films *All My Sons* and the very powerful *Key Largo*.

The 1950s saw Robinson's work-load decrease a little, although he did pop up to end a little *gravitas* to Cecil B DeMille's 1956 version of *The Ten Commandments*. In 1965, he gave one of his most memorable performances playing against the up-and-coming Steve McQueen in *The Cincinnati Kid*.

His parting shot, in the 1973 sci-fi thriller *Soylent Green*, saw him playing - with great dignity and pathos - an old man who chooses to submit to euthanasia. Remarkably,

Robinson never won an Oscar for any of his particular roles, although he was presented with a Special Academy Award in 1972 to recognize his contribution to the craft of film acting - which was considerable.

AUGUST 1
WALTER ULBRICHT - HARD MAN OF GERMANY

The man responsible for the Berlin Wall, for many years the most chilling symbol of the gulf between East and West and the opposing credos of communism and democracy, Walter Ulbricht - founder and leader of the German Communist Party - died today at the age of 80.

Born in Leipzig, Ulbricht was a trade union activist during World War I and helped found the Communist Party in 1919, becoming a member of Germany's parliament, the Reichstag, in 1928. Forced to flee Germany in 1933 with the rise of Hitler's Nazi Party, Ulbricht settled in the Soviet Union where his views were confirmed and hardened.

Returning to the Soviet-controlled East Germany in 1945, Ulbricht was effective head of the communist Socialist Unity Party from 1946 until his retirement in 1971 and - as Chairman of the Council of State in the German Democratic Republic from 1960 until his death - was the country's President in all but name.

A convinced Stalinist, despite all the evidence of brutality and excesses which emerged after the Russian dictator's death in 1953, Ulbricht was the single greatest obstacle to Germany's reunification, a stubborn and hard man who signalled his resistance to a settlement most dramatically in 1961 by ordering the erection of the Berlin Wall.

NOVEMBER 14

Royal Wedding Blows Britain's Blues Away

ECONOMIC PROBLEMS, oil shortages, political rows and the onset of winter were all forgotten for a few hours today as the British nation celebrated the marriage of Princess Anne to Captain Mark Phillips.

The full military ceremony – Captain Phillips wore the scarlet and blue uniform of the 1st Queen's Dragoon Guards – took place in Westminster Abbey before 1,500 guests. Thousands lined the streets of London to catch a glimpse of the happy couple while millions more watched what was the first royal wedding to be broadcast in colour on TV at home.

Princess Anne, who wore a high-necked wedding dress embroidered with pearls and silver thread, was attended by her younger brother, Prince Edward, and her cousin, Lady Sarah Armstrong-Jones.

After greeting a huge crowd from a Buckingham Palace balcony, the couple spent the first night of their honeymoon in the White House Lodge in Richmond Park before heading west to Barbados, for a fortnight aboard the Royal yacht Britannia.

1: Let Me In
- The Osmonds
2: Sorrow
- David Bowie
3: Daydreamer
/The Puppy Song
- David Cassidy
4: Top Of The World
- The Carpenters
5: Dyna-Mite
- Mud
6: Eye Level
- The Simon Park Level
7: I Love You Love
Me Love
- Gary Glitter
8: Ghetto Child
- The Detroit Spinners
9: For The Good Times
- Perry Como
10: Photograph
- Ringo Starr

NOVEMBER 25

Greek Colonels Stage Coup

Following the declaration of Martial Law in Athens last week, a group of Greek Army colonels supported by the armed forces, staged a coup today, toppling the government of President Papadopoulos in what seemed like a replay of the coup of 1967.

Today's coup appeared to have been bloodless, although armed troops were tonight patrolling the streets of Athens to enforce the curfew imposed by the new regime. The colonels' action followed continued unrest over civil liberties and political freedom in the eastern Mediterranean country. Earlier this month, nine people were said to have died in anti-government riots.

Uri Geller, Forkbender Extraordinaire

The phenomenon of Israeli psychic performer Uri Geller, 27, was introduced to the British public for the first time this month when, appearing on the Dimbleby *Talk-In* television programme, his psychokinetic powers appeared to bend viewers' cutlery and restart broken clocks and watches countrywide. BBC switchboards were jammed as Geller expounded on his supposedly extra-terrestrial gifts. And while tests appeared to disprove his belief in his own powers, he would remain an international celebrity of note.

NOVEMBER 26

Petrol Rationing Looms In Britain

The British Government today confirmed that petrol rationing coupons were being printed for issue to 16 million drivers next week. Coupon books were being distributed to post offices nationwide in an attempt to beat the Christmas rush, which was expected to clog the Royal Mail. As yet, no decision had been made on the introduction of rationing, although many petrol stations had run dry and been forced to close down.

A State of Emergency had been declared on November 13 when power workers and miners went on strike and the worldwide shortage of crude oil was exacerbated by oil companies hoarding stocks in case the Middle East crisis deepened. Plans were also drawn up to ensure that essential workers such as doctors, clergy, and public officials were given priority. In the US, President Nixon asked petrol stations to close on Sundays to reduce consumption and a 50 mph speed limit was imposed nationwide in a further bid to save vital fuel.

NOVEMBER 26

White House Tapes Contain 'Gaps'

In Washington, the Senate's Watergate hearings almost degenerated into farce when President Nixon's personal secretary, Miss Rose Mary Woods, related that she had made what she described as a 'terrible mistake' when she accidentally erased an 18-minute chunk of what had become known simply as 'The White House Tapes'.

Oddly enough, the missing part of the recording related to a conversation which the President had with his since-resigned aide, HR 'Bob' Haldeman, just three days after burglars broke in to the Democratic Party offices.

When Miss Woods told her boss that she'd accidentally pressed the wrong button, he apparently told her that it didn't matter. It was eventually discovered that there were a total of five crucial gaps in the tapes.

Soap Wars Hit British Screens

BRITISH TELEVISION VIEWERS gave programme chiefs something of a surprise this month when *Crossroads,* the critically-derided soap opera based in a Midlands motel, confirmed its status in the public's eye by notching three of the top five places in the monthly ratings – outgunning its nearest rival, the Manchester-set and filmed *Coronation Street* (pictured), behind which it had trailed badly in previous years.

Granada, the producers of *Coronation Street* who had refused to screen the rival in their region until 1970, would respond to the sudden threat by introducing a new girlfriend for one of their principal characters, Ken Barlow.

The newcomer, Elaine Perkins, was played by rising star Joanna Lumley who, in 1976, would create an even bigger impact as the glamorous special agent Purdey in *The New Avengers* and win awards a-plenty in the 1990s for her portrayal of Patsy in *Absolutely Fabulous*.

Ken Barlow, with whom Elaine parted after many rows (though matrimony had looked more than possible at one stage) remains in *Coronation Street* to this day, still played by actor William Roache. *Crossroads* would limp on after the 1981 departure of star Noele Gordon, but pack up its always-shaky sets in 1988.

Soviets Expelled From World Cup

In Geneva today, world soccer's governing body, FIFA, made the unprecedented decision to expel the Soviet Union from the World Cup soccer tournament for refusing to play a match against Chile. The Soviets justified their refusal, after a 0-0 draw with Chile in Moscow, by saying that the National Stadium in Santiago, the venue for the return game, had been used to house political prisoners during the recent right-wing coup. FIFA ruled the match should go ahead. When Chile took the field and the Soviet Union did not, the South Americans went through to the 1974 finals in West Germany.

Whitelaw Brokers Ulster Power-Sharing Deal

The British Secretary of State for Northern Ireland, Willie Whitelaw, was warmly received by both sides of the House of Commons today when he announced that moderate Catholics and Protestants in the Province had agreed to the formation of a coalition government to create a power-sharing executive. The new executive would oversee domestic administration in Northern Ireland, although the police and courts remained under the control of Westminster.

NOV

Crawford's Crackers – But The Show's A Hit!

THE BBC'S NEW situation comedy, *Some Mothers Do 'Ave Em,* proved an overnight smash when it was shown for the first time tonight, attracting viewers in nearly eight million homes and turning actor Michael Crawford into a household name.

Crawford's portrayal of the gormless, béret-clad Frank Spencer entered the acts of countless professional and amateur mimics, while the spectacular stunts (Crawford insisted on doing his own) were a feature of the show throughout both its successful series in 1973-74 and 1978.

The star would put his athleticism to full use when taking the title role in the London stage production of the musical *Barnum* in the 1980s, going on to reveal a hitherto under-appreciated side to his talents by singing extensively – and very well – in the Andrew Lloyd Webber musical *Phantom Of The Opera* in London and New York.

Gary Glitter - No 1 in the singles chart with *I Love You Love Me Love*

DECEMBER 28

Gulag Archipelago Published

The first of three volumes of Alexander Solzhenitsyn's semi-autobiographical *Gulag Archipelago,* which had been smuggled out of Russia as a hand-written manuscript, was published for the first time today in Paris. Solzhenitsyn, who suffered long years of internment in Siberian work camps, had finally exposed the full horrors of Stalinist Russia.

Already famous for his novels *One Day In the Life Of Ivan Denisovich* and *Cancer Ward,* both of which had caused the Soviet regime severe embarrassment, his epic 'history and geography' of Stalin's Soviet labour camps would result in his expulsion from Russia in 1974 - an exile which would not end until the Nobel Prize winning author finally returned in 1995.

DECEMBER 1

'Father of Israel' Ben-Gurion Dies

The nation of Israel went into renewed mourning today when David Ben-Gurion, one of its founding fathers, died in Tel Aviv at the age of 87. Ben-Gurion, Born David Green in Russia, Ben-Gurion was elected the first Prime Minister of Israel in 1948, serving until 1953 and again from 1955 to 1963. As Prime Minister, he oversaw the growth of Israel into an democratic country with an international reputation. In later years, the man who had been a hot-blooded freedom-fighter in his youth, spent much of his time in writing and studying.

Although he went to what some might describe as extreme lengths to study the Old Testament by learning Greek at the age of 56, he subsequently studied Sanskrit in order to expand his knowledge of Buddhism!

DECEMBER 3

Jupiter's Secrets Unlocked By Pioneer 10

As it flew by Jupiter today, NASA's *Pioneer 10* - the first spacecraft to be sent to one of the solar system's large outer planets, probed the planet's radiation belts, took many photographs, including several of its satellites, and established that electron bursts detected near Earth were actually coming from Jupiter. It then mapped the planet's large magnetic field, expanding and contracting in response to pressure from solar winds. Continuing onwards, *Pioneer 10* later disclosed solar phenomena from beyond the orbit of Pluto, which it would cross in April 1983 at a distance from Earth of more than 4.3 billion km (2.7 billion miles), the furthest an Earth-made spacecraft had travelled, and well beyond its predicted 21-month life.

DECEMBER 13

Three-Day Week A Harsh Reality

BRITISH MINE UNION leaders' decision to continue their ban on overtime working without taking a ballot of members precipitated today's move by Prime Minister Edward Heath to put the country on a three-day working week. Industrial plants and other work-places would henceforth find their electricity supplies limited to only three working days, and TV broadcasts would end at 10.30 every evening.

In an effort to reduce public demand for imported goods in the face of increased OPEC oil prices, Chancellor Anthony Barber tightened credit controls, but refrained from increasing VAT, in a crisis budget. He also slashed £1,200 million off public spending - a move attacked by Shadow Chancellor Denis Healey, who said the rich should be taxed more.

As the year drew to a disastrous close, it was clear that Mr Heath - who had recently asked the not-so rhetorical question 'Who rules the country, an elected government or the unions?' - would probably need to call a snap general election in the New Year to secure a strong new mandate for his fight.

His discomfort was not eased by news that, in Uganda, President Idi Amin had set up a 'Save Britain' fund in a tongue-in-cheek effort to help the UK out of its economic mess.

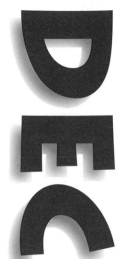

DECEMBER 6

Arab–US Money War Escalates

In Britain, £2,000 million was wiped off the value of shares on the London Stock Exchange today - the worst one-day fall since World War II - when Arab funds were withdrawn from Western banks, the result of a 'money war' between the United States and the Arab League.

The attack plan drawn up by Arab economists was aimed at using the vast money reserves of Middle Eastern countries to fund development projects in the region. It was also another effective way of punishing the US for its support of Israel in the recent war. Total Arab money thought to be on deposit in the West amounted to $10 billion, more than 10 per cent of which was held by British banks.

DECEMBER 30

Marks & Spencer Boss Shot

The Middle East war reached London today when Joseph Sieff, head of the Marks & Spencer department store chain and one of Britain's leading Jewish public figures, was shot and badly wounded by gunmen thought to be linked with the anti-Israeli group, Black September.

Sixty-eight-year old Mr Sieff was well-known for his support for Zionist causes and had received death threats in the past. He was attacked in his London home in St John's Wood. Rushed to hospital, surgeons carried out an operation to remove a bullet from his jaw.

DECEMBER 20

Spanish Premier Assassinated

The Basque terrorist group ETA claimed responsibility for the death of Admiral Luis Carrero Blanco, the Spanish Prime Minister, in a car bomb attack today in Madrid.

Six terrorists were thought to have planted the bomb, which exploded next to the church where the Prime Minister had just attended Mass. His car was hurled into the air by the massive blast and landed on a second-floor balcony.

Although Admiral Blanco, who was 70, was carried alive from the remains of his vehicle, he died shortly afterwards in hospital, the latest and most prominent victim of Basque extremists fight to win their region independence from Spain.

YOUR 1973 HOROSCOPE

Unlike most Western horoscope systems which group astrological signs into month-long periods based on the influence of 12 constellations, the Chinese believe that those born in the same year of their calendar share common qualities, traits and weaknesses with one of 12 animals - Rat, Ox, Tiger, Rabbit, Dragon, Snake, Horse, Sheep, Monkey, Rooster, Dog or Pig.

They also allocate the general attributes of five natural elements - Earth, Fire, Metal, Water, Wood - and an overall positive or negative aspect to each sign to summarize its qualities.

If you were born between January 16, 1972 and February 2, 1973, you are a Rat. As this book is devoted to the events of 1973, let's take a look at the sign which governs those born between February 3 that year and January 22, 1974 - The Year of The Ox:

THE OX
FEBRUARY 15, 1961
- FEBRUARY 4, 1962
ELEMENT: METAL   ASPECT: (-)

Oxen individuals are solid, even stolid characters with strong personalities. Trustworthy and dependable, they seek integrity and always face their responsibilities. They are kind, caring souls, full of common sense and very down to earth. Very preoccupied with security, they are ready to work long and hard to provide a nest for themselves.

Despite this need for security, Oxen are also strong-minded, individualistic - and don't take kindly to being told what to do. They are, in fact, quite dominant and have high standards of excellence, like to make rules and tend to dislike those who step out of line. They have to learn to be more tolerant of those around them if they want to live in a peaceful environment.

Oxen are quiet, steady and methodical, preferring to to be in the background rather than be pushed to the front. However, they can display leadership qualities when necessary, adopting a commanding presence and an ability to take charge. They easily earn the respect and loyalty of others.

Even though they don't like to be in the limelight, the Oxen's strong-minded willpower and conscientious attitude will see them to the top, sooner or later. Practical, conservative and traditional, they believe in building things bit by bit, and always based on solid ground. They can be very stylish and individualistic in the way they look, and know how to present themselves.

Oxen are very affectionate to those close to their hearts, but quite cool and distant with strangers. Once Oxen commit themselves, they're loyal, deep and passionate, even if they seem to lack originality and romance. But they also have a tendency to retreat into themselves when they suffer, and don't cry out their emotions.

Oxen are conservative in many aspects of life, but for them conservatism goes with emotion and commitment. They like to build solid, secure foundations in life and plan everything carefully. Hard work, tenacity and loyalty take them to the top, where Oxen enjoy being quietly dominant.

FAMOUS OXEN

HRH The Princess of Wales
Richard Nixon
former President of the United States
Margaret Thatcher
former Prime Minister of Britain
Jane Fonda
Oscar-winning actress, former political activist

Robert Redford
Oscar-winning actor, director, conservationist
Dustin Hoffman
Oscar-winning actor, noted perfectionist
Twiggy
model, actress, singer
Fatima Whitbread
former world javelin champion